soul
fitness

with Frederick D. Haynes III

D0396035

FREDERICK D. HAYNES III

Patricia Benjamin Webb, compiler

soul
fitness
with Frederick D. Haynes III

JUDSON PRESS
PUBLISHERS SINCE 1824

VALLEY FORGE, PA

Soul Fitness with Frederick D. Haynes III

Judson Press has made every effort to trace the ownership of all quotes. In the event of a question arising from the use of a quote, we regret any error made and will be pleased to make the necessary correction in future printings and editions of this book.

Bible quotations in this volume are from *The Holy Bible*, King James Version (KJV); THE MESSAGE, copyright © 1993, 1994, 1995, used by permission of NavPress Publishing Group (*The Message*); HOLY BIBLE: *New International Version*, copyright © 1973, 1978, 1984, used by permission of Zondervan (NIV); the *Holy Bible,* New Living Translation, copyright © 1996, used by permission of Tyndale House Publishers, Inc., Wheaton, IL 60189, all rights reserved (NLT); and the New Revised Standard Version of the Bible, copyright © 1989 by the Division of Christian Education of the National Council of the Churches of Christ in the United States of America, used by permission, all rights reserved (NRSV).

Library of Congress Cataloging-in-Publication Data
Haynes, Frederick D., 1960-
Soul fitness with Frederick D. Haynes III / Frederick D. Haynes III; Patricia Benjamin Webb, compiler. — 1st ed.
p. cm.
ISBN 978-0-8170-1519-0 (pbk. : alk. paper) 1. Christian life. I. Webb, Patricia Benjamin. II. Title.   BV4510.3.H39 2007
248.4—dc22

2007013964

Printed on recycled paper in the U.S.A.

Second Edition, 2008.

To Aunt Reetee,
a kind, loving, appreciative, talented,
sincere servant child of God

"I just want to make God look good!"
—Serita Sue Doyle Lattimore

Special Thanks to
FDH Ministries Book Project Team,
especially Cynthia White,
CD transcription project leader
Dwala Brown, transcriber

Contents

Foreword

In one of the old hymns of the church, "A Charge to Keep I Have," the songwriter says in one of the verses:

> To serve this present age, my calling to fulfill
> May it all my powers engage to do my
> Master's Will.

What the hymnodist is saying—or really, *praying*—is for the grace to use all the gifts God has given him to do God's will and to serve the generation in which he finds himself. What a powerful truth is wrapped up in the words of that hymn.

We cannot serve our parents' generation. We cannot serve our grandparents' generation. We cannot serve our great-grandparents' generation. We can learn from the rich legacy they leave us. We can drink deep from the fountains of wisdom that they filled for us, but we cannot equip them to live back in their day or equip them to live in the future. Their day has passed!

The real task in ministry is to find ways to serve the people who are our contemporaries. The difficult challenge in saying yes to God's call upon your life is to find ways to address the realities of life with which those who live around you and those among who you live face everyday of their lives. That is what "serving this present age" means.

That is exactly and precisely what Rev. Dr. Frederick Douglas Haynes does. Freddy speaks to "this present age." He takes the rich gospel of Jesus Christ and translates it into a language that the people who live in the twenty-first century can understand. Freddy takes the gospel out of the dusty pages of the seventeenth century King James Version and translates it into language that the hip hop generation understands.

Freddy takes the truths that are locked in the dusty halls of holy history, lifts them out of the pages of the Bible, and transports them from Galilee, Palestine, Northeast Africa, and Greece into Dallas, Texas, Los Angeles, California, Chicago, Illinois, New York, New York, and Miami, Florida!

Jesus served his "present age." He talked in terms that those around him could understand. He used illustrations from their daily lives. He talked about a farmer planting seeds. He talked about a man having two sons whose personalities were radically different. (Everybody with children could relate to that one!) Jesus talked about a brother having his stuff jacked and being left for dead by some gangbangers who needed the financial resources to buy or sell drugs! The man whose passions had been jacked was left for dead in the heart of the hood and the church folk would not help him. Every poor person, every homeless person, and every person kicked to the curb by first century Palestinian culture resonated with what Jesus was saying in that story.

Jesus spoke to his "present age" so effectively that the Bible says, "The common people heard Him gladly!" Jesus did not use heavy theological terms, deep philosophical concepts, and complicated epistemological constructs to speak to everyday people about the love of God, the grace of God, the will of God, and the ways of God. Jesus used language they could understand.

Freddy Haynes does the same thing. Freddy takes the words of Jay-Z, the songs of Luther Vandross, the raps of Kanye West and Common, the expressions of Snoop Dog, and the lyrics of Beyonce to articulate the gospel of Jesus Christ to a generation of young people who were not raised in the church.

Indeed, because Freddy uses all the "powers" God has given him to speak to this present age, there are thousands who have come to know Christ, confess Christ, and led to join a local congregation—in large part because of Dr. Haynes' translation of the Good News into language to which and with which they can relate!

Dr. John W. Kinney, dean of the Samuel DeWitt Proctor School of Theology at Virginia Union University, tells the story of how the most effective teacher he had in his many years of training was not a theologian in New York. The most effective teacher John had was an old woman in his congregation who had not been to college.

John not only finished college and graduate school with a bachelor's degree and a Master of Divinity. John also has a PhD that is an earned *dual* degree from Columbia University and Union Theological Seminary in New York. John's area of concentration is philosophical theology.

When Dr. Kinney came home from graduation with that fully earned and highly prized PhD in his hand, he preached what he thought was one of the most powerful sermons in the history of homiletics. After church, the old woman in his congregation said to him, "Son? You have got a rich and full fountain bubbling over in your breast. God has put it there and it will nourish the souls of countless thousands in generations to come. If you want me to drink from this fountain that God has given you, however…if you want me to drink from this fountain that is bubbling inside of you…if you want me to be nourished by the healing and living waters that are flowing from the well and the wellspring of your soul, then the next time you preach, put this water that God has given you in a cup that I can recognize!"

Dr. Haynes offers the living waters that Jesus spoke of in John 4 and that John Kinney's member spoke of in Beaver Dam, Virginia, and Dr. Haynes puts that water into a cup that this present age can recognize! Pastor Haynes' daily meditations on K104.5 FM have served this present age. His preaching each week at Friendship-West Baptist Church in Dallas has served this present age. His revival work from Seattle to San Diego, from Detroit to New

Orleans and from Maine to Miami, has served this present age.

As you read the meditations in *Soul Fitness,* you will find the fiber of your faith strengthened. You will also see a minister of the gospel being faithful in offering all his gifts and talents to God to be a blessing in the lives of those among whom God has placed him in "this present age."

REV. DR. JEREMIAH A. WRIGHT JR.
Pastor, Trinity United Church of Christ
Chicago, Illinois

Introduction

Each morning on K104 FM, the number one urban contemporary morning radio show in Dallas–Fort Worth, Texas, Dr. Frederick D. Haynes III shares his daily intravenous (IV) shot of inspiration to thousands of listeners. His message is the number one requests on the station's website. His messages reach and impact people ages 5–65.

Subjects range from Coretta Scott King to Hurricane Katrina to Kanye West. Themes encompass each individual's relationship with God, with neighbor, and with self. This book is a collection of reflections based on those radio messages delivered in 2005–06. May these intravenous doses of spiritual vitamins provide a jumpstart for your day, a boost of fitness for your soul, and revitalized strength to make a difference in your life, your church, your community, and the world.

1. Fitness for Your Soul

During the winter season most people get sick. They get a cold; they get the flu. Often we set ourselves up to be taken down by one of these diseases because our resistance is low. We run and run until our body is run down, and as a consequence, our body gives out—and we give up. So we need to stay physically fit in order to keep up our resistance.

Isn't it also true that, every now and then, we get run down in *life*? Life runs you down until you just don't have any more strength. Not just physically; I'm also talking about emotionally, spiritually, and psychologically. You feel like, *Hey, I can't take this anymore.* You are run down. Why? Because your resistance is down. I want to encourage you today to keep up your resistance.

This book is called *Soul Fitness* because only by fortifying your physical, emotional, spiritual, and mental resistance will you have power to carry on in life and ministry. Physically, you do that by taking vitamins, getting plenty of rest, eating right, and exercising. That's common knowledge. But what about maintaining your emotional, mental, and spiritual fitness?

Here are some basic principles for achieving "soul fitness." First, every now and then you need to take time to take *in* you what you need to give *out*. You can't just give and give and give, or ultimately you are going to *burn* out. Every now and then you have to receive something internally that will energize and inspire you. That's why I thank God for the brilliance of Dallas radio personality Skip Murphy, who said, "Every day we need to have an IV." Here's what Murphy means.

If you want to increase your intake of nourishment for your soul, *pray*. Talk to God. *Read* the Scriptures. Open up God's Word. Then take time to *meditate* on what you have read and talked about with God. These three practices—what the church calls *disciplines*—have a powerful way of putting *in*side of you what you need to handle things *out*side of you. These habits will fill you inside so you can handle what's outside. They will lift you when life is trying to drag you down and weaken your resistance.

Second, after taking in the soul nourishment you need, sometimes you should also call time-out for yourself and just chill. That's right—just chill. You don't have to make

2

You have to say, "Your issue is not going to be my issue. I'm *not* going to hold a grudge. I'm going to forgive you."

every meeting; you don't have to do it all and be it all for everyone. If you aren't there, I promise, life will go on. So on occasion you have to say, "No, I can't do that right now. I'm going to take time for myself." Call time-out and chill out.

Finally, there are some things you need to let go of altogether. You need to stop carrying some of the baggage you've been toting. What kind of baggage? Other people's issues and other people's actions. Grudges and bitterness for wrongs done to you. You have to say, "Your issue is not going to be my issue. I'm *not* going to hold a grudge. I'm going to forgive you." Some things you just need to let go.

I want you to have a healthy day, a healthy month, a healthy year. I want you to experience complete soul fitness. But if you are going to enjoy physical, emotional, mental, and spiritual fitness, then you have to keep up your resistance and get soul fit!

2. Keep it Real

Please don't make the mistake of living your life by trying to make everybody else happy. People will have their agendas for you, but if you spend all your life trying to make everybody else happy, guess what. You are going to spend your life unhappy.

You cannot live *down* to others' expectations, or you will never live *up* to your own expectations. See, I've discovered people are always going to have something to say. People who have *no* business are going to make it *their* business to get into *your* business. People are going to hate. Folks are going to speculate. So in a real sense, if you're not careful, you will spend all your life chasing after somebody else's expectations only to fail to live up to your own expectations. It is no wonder Shakespeare said back in the day, "This above all: To thine own self be true, and it must follow, as the night the day, thou canst not then be false to any man."[1]

I came across a wonderful story about Pastor Bob Olmstead from Reno, Nevada. Pastor Olmstead was driving along the road one day and spotted a wounded bird on the pavement. Cars were whizzing past it. The pastor saw the bird and helped it because he knew it would otherwise eventually get hit by a car. He stopped his car, jumped out, and stopped traffic the best he could. The other drivers were ticked. Traffic was backing up. Some people were honking their horns. Others were giving him half a peace sign! They all were wondering what this foolish man was doing.

Pastor Olmstead was doing everything he could to catch the bird! He was running here and there, but the bird, of course, was afraid of him and, though wounded, kept running from him. And he realized that in spite of all he was trying to do to help the bird, everybody else was getting angry. Why? Finally it dawned on the pastor that no one else could see what he could see. They could not see the wounded bird.

I saw another lesson in Pastor Olmstead's story. It occurred to me that he was being true to himself. Keeping it real with himself. Recognizing that even though nobody else could see what he saw, he couldn't leave that wounded bird on the highway to face certain death under the wheels of the next speeding car.

You cannot live *down* to others' expectations, or you will never live *up* to your own expectations.

Isn't that the way it is in life? Not everybody can see what you see. Why? Because most people haven't been given the vision that you have been given. So, you have to keep it real with yourself and you will discover three truths.

1. When you are real with yourself, fake people can't hang with you.

2. When you are real with yourself, that's when you are truly free and you are empowered.

3. Never forget, when you keep it real with yourself, God is holding you responsible for being the you that God made you and nobody else.

In his day Shakespeare said, "To thine own self be true." I'll spin it this way: "Keep it real with yourself."

Note
1. William Shakespeare, *Hamlet*, Act 1, scene iii, lines 78–80.

6

3. Born to Be a Baller

Some people never do their best because they are convinced they don't deserve any better. So, as a consequence, they just go through life settling. They settle for a dead-end career; they settle for an abusive relationship; they settle for a lifestyle beneath their potential. They're cool with mediocrity. Their lives are just full of the same-old, same-old. And you look at them and you know they should be doing better. But if *they* don't believe they deserve better, then they will never try to do better in any area of their lives. But I'm convinced we can all be ballers. We should all be playing, or living, our best game. Here's why.

A while ago I watched a local television news anchor, John McCaa, doing a piece on Oscar-nominated actor

Allow the majesty that's already been placed in you to come out of you, and people will follow you.

Terrence Howard, who was starring at the time in his latest movie, *Hustle and Flow.* Howard talked about getting ready for this role as a pimp who was searching for his true calling. So Howard went out and interviewed some pimps, one of whom dropped a bomb on him. This guy said, "If you want to be a great pimp, you have to allow the majesty in you to come out of you. Then people will follow you."

That blew my mind because it is wisdom from, of all persons, a pimp! Of course, he's in the wrong kind of life, but I have to hand it to him because he's on to something. Allow the majesty that's already been placed in you to come out of you, and people will follow you.

That's my challenge to you today. Recognize that God has placed majesty in you. Allow it to come out of you. You'll blow up and be the baller[1] that God intends you to be. Is that a little too much flava for you? Well, let me give you the word in the Word.

The Bible says in 1 Peter 2:9, "But you are a chosen race, a royal priesthood, a holy nation, God's own people" (NRSV). In other words, you are a child of the King. And when you are a child of the King, there is royalty in you. Allow the royalty, the majesty, to come out of you, and you'll be the person God intends for you to be.

So remember these three things: (1) When God made you, it wasn't an accident. God created you with intent. So make sure you fulfill God's divine arrangement, and allow the royalty and majesty in you to come out. (2) Never settle for less than God's best for you. God deserves it, and so do you. And (3) recognize that in this life you are a partner with God's providence. God made you with anointed imagination, stepped back, patted himself on the back, and said, "That's good!"

You were born to be a baller, so allow the majesty in you to come on out.

Note

1. *Baller* originally referred to the guys who grew up on the streets in the 'hood and made it big in professional basketball. Nowadays, the word is used to describe anyone (including the pimp-turned-DJ played by Howard) who rises from the bottom of the ladder to live large at the top.

4. Finding God When You've Lost it All

Have you ever felt like you were just losing it because of what you have lost? Every now and then, we lose something or someone, and if we're not careful, we can "lose it"—psychologically, physically, or spiritually.

For example, when you lose your job, you feel like going off the deep end. When a loved one dies, you may feel you can't continue living. When a relationship you've invested your heart and your hope in, your life and your love in, is suddenly snatched away, that's cause to make you want to quit on love. All of us have lost something or someone. And when we lose that thing or one, the loss seems much larger, much more encompassing than it is. We sometimes feel we have lost it all.

If you can identify with that feeling, take a moment to think about those people in Alabama, Louisiana, and Mississippi after Hurricane Katrina. I called a friend of mine who lived in New Orleans and was finally able to make contact with him. I was blown away by his wonderful spirit and testimony. When the hurricane came, he started to gather all of his things, thinking he'd leave. Then he discovered something he thought he had lost. It was a Bible that had been given to him by his late grandmother. When he picked up the Bible, the pages fell open to this passage: "When thou passest through the waters, I will be with thee; and through the rivers, they shall not overflow thee: when thou walkest through the fire, thou shalt not be burned" (Isaiah 43:2, KJV).

When he read that Scripture, my friend decided to stay right where he was, and as a consequence, he has really gone through it and come out a better man. He said to me, "Pastor Haynes, let me share these things with you. First, I'm still here. God is good. And I discovered something. What I've lost I can replace, but what I found is what I really can't get along without."

Is that not a powerful testimony of how you can find God even in the midst of losing it all? What does my friend teach us? First, I don't care what you've lost; *you're still here*. The bottom line is you're still standing; you're still breathing; you haven't lost your mind. God still has a purpose for you. Your life is filled with possibilities and potential. Say it out loud: "I'm still here!"

"What I've lost I can replace, but what I found is what I really can't get along without."

Then my friend said, "What I've lost I can replace." God is in the business of blessing you to profit from your losses. My friend lost some stuff, but everything he lost could be replaced. He had insurance, so he could profit from his losses. If you look back over your life, some of the stuff you've lost, some of the people you've lost, God has replaced all of it with things and people that are even better for you. Why? Because God is the only one I know who can turn a loss into a profit.

Finally, my friend made a discovery in the midst of his disaster. What he found was the Word of God. In finding the Word of God, he reconnected with God. And as a consequence, he is closer to God. I've discovered that whenever you think you have lost it all, that's exactly when you find almighty God. You can find God when you've lost it all.

5. Got to Give It Up

What are you holding on to? Is there anything behind you that's keeping you from what God has before you? A lot of us get stuck in this life. Stuck like Chuck in bad situations; stuck like Chuck on stupid. We're stuck in a situation we need to escape, but somehow we can't let go. If you're not careful, you may hold on to what you need to let go of and miss out on the good God has planned for you.

The other day I was watching the news on TV. At the bottom was this running banner that highlights certain news stories from around the world. That day the news item was about a woman in Kentucky who had been rescued from a fire in her home. She had been rescued, but she went back into the fire to retrieve her cat. When she went back into the house, she lost her life. She perished in the fire because she

Do you keep going back to what God has already delivered you from? . . . You've got to give it up!

went back to what she had been delivered from. She went back because of something she could not let go.

Do you keep going back to what God has already delivered you from? What is it that you can't let go? What is keeping you from the future God has for you?

What do you have to give up? One, you have to give up *hostility*. What are you hostile about? Has someone done something to you? Some of us go through life not understanding there is danger in uncontrolled anger. Give up that hostility so you don't miss out on God's possibilities.

Two, you have to give up your *hurts*. Once you give up those hurts, you'll discover that God uses what hurts you in order to help you. It is just as the saying goes: what doesn't kill you will make you stronger.

Three, you have to give up your *history* because it's getting in the way and keeping you from receiving the future God has for you. The woman lost her life because she went back to what she had been delivered from—because of what she could not let go. She was clinging to her history.

You've got to give it up. The apostle Paul puts it like this: "Forgetting what is behind and straining toward what is ahead, I press on toward the goal to win the prize for which God has called me heavenward in Christ Jesus" (Philippians 3:13-14, NIV). You've got to give it up.

6. Falling UP

We've all blown it, messed up, made some dumb decisions, stayed stuck on stupid far too long. A lot of us have turned left when we should have turned right. Yeah, we've all made some choices we wish we could take back. We've gone places we wish we had not gone with people we wish we had never hooked up with. The bottom line is that we all have failed. The question is, when you fail do you fail by falling down or falling up?

I learned this lesson from my daughter, Abeni. I was talking to her last night on the phone, and she was telling me about her day. She told me, "Daddy, I fell up the stairs."

"What do you mean by that?" I asked.

She replied, "I was running up the steps, and I fell."

I said, "What do you mean?"

She repeated, "I fell up the steps."

What Abeni was trying to describe was that when she was running up the steps, she tripped and missed a step, but guess what? She landed on a level higher than she had been before she began her fall. Abeni said to me as I began to mess with her, "Well, at least I fell up!"

I like that. "At least I fell up!" I did not fall back; I did not fall down, but I fell up. That's a beautiful thing, because that's the key to really living: to recognize that all of us are going to blow it, mess up, fail. All of us are going to let ourselves down. All of us are going to disappoint ourselves. But the good news is, when you fall like Abeni, you fall up.

That's my question for you today. Not *will* you fail, but *when* you fail, are you going to fall down or are you going to fall up? I love that challenge, and it offers two lessons I'll pass on to you. First, it dawned on me that failure is not final and it does not have to be fatal, but it can be fruitful. How so? Failure can be fruitful if it *develops* you but does not *define* you.

You see, if you're not careful, when you fail (as we all do) you will define yourself as a failure. But no, you're not a failure; you just happened to fail this time. Understand there is a difference between failing and being a failure. If you define yourself as a failure, then sadly failure becomes final, and it may even become fatal. But check this: failure does not have to be final or fatal. It can be fruitful if you allow it to *develop* you but not *define* you. There are some

Failure can be fruitful if it *develops* you but does not *define* you.

things you can learn from failure that you cannot learn from success. Failure can be a real good teacher, so in a real sense, failure can be fruitful.

That brings us to lesson two, and this ought to bless you. The reason failure can be fruitful is because God is a God of another chance. Don't you thank God for that? Even when we've been bad, God is still good. God is a God of another chance who *makes up* where we *messed up,* so we end up *blessed* up. Isn't that a beautiful thought—that through all the mess and all the bad choices, somehow we end up on a higher level because God is a God of another chance? And that's my word today. You will certainly stumble and fall in this life, but the question is, when you fall, will you fall up?

7. A Big Break from a Bad Break

We all know a bad break can break you. Some of you even go through your whole life broken by bad breaks. The bottom line is that bad breaks show up on the itinerary of every individual who is making a pilgrimage on this planet. So all of you know something about bad breaks.

Just when you think you're about to get everything together, you get a bad report from the doctor; something is wrong with your health. That's a bad break. You invest your money in something you believe is going to give you a great return, only to lose all that you have invested. That's a bad break. Bad breaks on the job, bad breaks in a relationship—all of us have had these experiences. We think everything is going to be right—it ends up all wrong. Bad breaks.

God uses your *dis*appointments as *divine* appointments so you can make a new *discovery*.

I once read that in 1915 Coffee County, Alabama, was invaded by the dreaded boll weevil. This community was in the heart of the cotton belt, and the boll weevil stripped the cotton of its leaves and stole the entire community's livelihood. The whole community faced starvation. They had a bad break.

But instead of caving in, the community invited an African American scientist, George Washington Carver, to come to the county. And he told them, in so many words, don't just get stuck on stupid and be upset because you lost your cotton crop. Your soil is still good for harvesting peanuts. And you know what happened? They were able to harvest a peanut crop and rescue their community from economic disaster.

Then they erected a statue in the middle of Coffee County, Alabama—to the boll weevil! Why? Because the boll weevil had given them a bad break that set the stage for them to have a big break.

In this life all of us will have bad breaks. The question is what you will do when you have a bad break. First, do what Mariah Carey says. Learn to shake it off or it will tear you down. That's number one: shake it off.

Second, God uses each of your *dis*appointments as *divine* appointments so you can make a new *discovery*.

That's number two: see your disappointments as something God can use to give you a divine appointment.

Third, what goes *wrong* can set you up for what is *right*. What seems like a bad break might just be God's way of getting you what God has been trying to get for you all along. That's number three: See what can be *right* in the *wrong*.

Bottom line? All of us have bad breaks, but when God is in your life, God has a way of taking your bad breaks and using them to set you up for your big breaks.

8. God Planted You– Now Bloom There!

If you want to waste good energy, spend your time lusting after what other people have. Spend all your time comparing and complaining and whining. That's where *hateration*—my word for a combination of hatred and envy—comes from. When you spend all your time looking at what others have instead of focusing on what you have, you create hateration in yourself.

Instead, your motto ought to be: God has planted me right where I am. My responsibility is to bloom here.

I first heard that idea spoken by legendary preacher Dr. C. A. W. Clark of Dallas, Texas. Dr. Clark was preaching one day and said, "If you are just a lemon, and God made somebody else a peach, here's what you do. Add some sugar to your situation and make some lemonade. God has planted you, so blossom right where you are." But what does that mean?

First, it means you ought to invest your *best* in yourself. What kind of energy are you investing in yourself? What do I mean by that? Simply recognize that in this life you deserve the best. If you deserve the best, then you deserve to invest your best in yourself. God has planted you. Blossom and bloom where you are.

Second, God is so good that the Holy Spirit is up to something in your life right now, right where you are. God says you don't have to go to another place or find another person to experience happiness. Happiness can be right where you are. It's within you. God has planted you. Blossom right where you are.

Finally, recognize that God knows exactly what you need to bloom. God has a way of giving you *what* you need *when* you need it so you can blossom and become everything God wants you to be. Like Dr. Clark used to say, "Quit trying to find your happiness in somebody else."

Stop being jealous of what somebody else has. Discover that, in order for you to be all that God intends for you, everything you need is either already placed inside you or—watch this!—it's on its way to you. God has reservations for you in the land called Greatness, *if* you recognize that God has planted you. Bloom right where you are.

9. I Can't Let This Keep Me Down

Life can go wrong, and when it goes wrong, it's hard to feel right. As a matter of fact, life can go so wrong that it can knock you down. When life knocks you down, you might find yourself staying down. So much so that you conclude that down is best for you. One old blues song put it this way: "I've been down so long 'til down don't bother me no more." Evidently that comes from someone who had been knocked down, had become used to being down, and thought that down was his or her destiny.

One night after the Dallas Cowboys (sadly) lost a football game, Coach Parcells spoke about the loss, saying, "This is one of those things that can really linger if you're not careful." When I heard that, it dawned on me—isn't that what happens in life? When things don't work out the way we want them to, we find ourselves surrendering to the situation and lingering on it. Something that was already bad suddenly becomes worse. Why? Because not only have you experienced a crushing defeat, but if you're not careful, it can get into your spirit, mess with your mind, break your heart, and make you conclude there's nothing you can do.

"I've been down so long, down don't bother me no more." But my word to you is simple: You don't have to stay down! You can get back up!

My grandmother used to say something to me that really blessed me. She said, "When life knocks you down the best thing to do is to look up. Because when you look up, you will get up." I learned something heavy from that. I learned not to focus on what I have lost, but to focus on what's left over. What you have left over is what will give you the creativity to rebuild your life again.

Grandma also taught me that when you get knocked down in this life and you look up, you will end up going where you're looking. So make sure you look where you're going! I like that, because life is about *outlook*. It's not about what happens to you. It's about how you *see* what happens to you. So make sure that when you're knocked down, you look up, because when you look up, then you'll get up.

Remember, down is not your destiny. God has too much of a future in store for you. What happens to you does not have to be the last word on you. If you look up, the next

...life is about *outlook*....It's about how you *see* what happens to you.

thing you will do is get up. Weeping may endure for a night but joy is coming in the morning (see Psalm 30:5). You will get up because, as the Bible tells us: "Even the youths shall faint and be weary, and the young men shall utterly fall: But they that wait upon the LORD shall renew their strength; they shall mount up with wings as eagles; they shall run, and not be weary; and they shall walk, and not faint" (Isaiah 40:30-31, KJV).

Just because life knocks you down, that doesn't mean you have to stay down.

10. God Wants to Hook You Up

There's nothing worse in life than feeling disconnected. Have you ever felt empty? Unfulfilled? That is disconnected—when you feel no connection with yourself and no connection with God, and then it's hard to feel connected to somebody else.

I heard a story about some gypsies who were at a conference in the Middle East. These gypsies were desert dwellers, but at this conference they stayed in a beautiful hotel and were blown away by a faucet in their room. Coming from the faucet was the precious resource known as water.

When these desert dwellers saw water coming from this faucet, they believed all their problems would be solved if they could just take the faucet back to the desert. So they unscrewed the faucet and took it home to the desert. They told all their friends to gather around, and then they turned the knobs. Of course, nothing came out. Why? Because in spite of how beautiful the faucet looked, it was disconnected from the *source* that gave it *re*source.

And that's what I'm saying to you. When you move through life disconnected, you don't have the resources to make it. Now here's the good news. We serve a God who is so good he wants to hook you up with all that's good, and when God hooks you up, God blesses you.

First of all, God blesses you with *peace* because God is a God of peace. When God's peace gets in you, then you become a person of peace as well. That means other folks can't drag you into their drama. When you are *at* peace, you won't let anyone treat you like *a* piece. That's why Paul said the peace of God passes all understanding (see Philippians 4:7)—because if you've never experienced it, you can't possibly comprehend it.

Second, when God hooks you up with divine blessings, God gives you *purpose*. There is no better feeling in life than to know you are doing the will of almighty God. When you are *doing* God's will, you are *in* God's will, and when you are *in* God's will, you are *connected* with your purpose. When you are connected with your purpose, you will wake up every day knowing that your life is not an accident but an appointment and that you are operating under divine assignment.

When you are *at* peace, you won't let anyone treat you like *a* piece.

Because I've been hooked up by God, I have peace, I have purpose, and finally, I have *power*. When God hooks you up, you have power. Power from within to be all you can be, do all God wants you to do, and say with the apostle Paul, "I can do everything with the help of Christ who gives me the strength I need" (Philippians 4:13, NLT).

Paul was simply saying that God had hooked him up. That's my word to you today. Don't live life disconnected, because there is a God who has nothing but love for you, and that God wants to hook you up.

11. Do the Doggone Thing

The Bible says in James 2:26 that "faith without works is dead" (KJV). In other words, don't just pray for somebody. Move beyond prayer to touch hearts, change lives, and make a difference. God has been good *to* you because God wants to be good *through* you. Let me give you some examples.

At my church, Friendship-West Baptist, we served lunch to some brothers and sisters from Katrina-ravaged New Orleans, whom we called our honored guests. We didn't refer to them or treat them as refugees. They were our honored guests. They had been through a lot, but they were strong. The fact that they had survived was evidence that God was not through with them. Even more amazing, however, was our discovery that God wanted to use us to

Move beyond prayer to touch hearts, change lives, and make a difference.

work with them and be a blessing through them. Calling them refugees would have dehumanized them. They were honored guests who deserved to be treated with dignity and class. They deserved to have housing and appropriate shelter, not to be warehoused and given prison blankets. They deserved to be our honored guests.

Nearby Mount Tabor Baptist Church had those same guests for dinner every evening—and we weren't the only two congregations getting involved. Soon there was a meeting for all pastors and church leaders in the city manager's office downtown because we wanted to coordinate our efforts. If we coordinated, we would all be on the same page to help our honored guests get the services they needed.

We also issued a challenge to all of our businesses, motels, and hotels. We wanted to put our guests into housing, into appropriate venues where they could experience the dignity they deserved. We asked everyone to step up, to do the right thing—and that meant, not charging these honored guests. Hurricane Katrina was a major national crisis, and we needed all hands on deck, not just united in prayer but moving beyond prayer to change lives and make a difference.

We still need those hands. More than a year after Katrina, much of New Orleans and many other communities along the Gulf are still devastated. Many residents are still displaced. Neighborhoods are virtual ghost towns. And the federal, state, and local governments have been largely ineffective in bringing any kind of restoration to the people and places ravaged by the floodwaters.

It isn't only the post-Katrina Gulf region. It's the rural areas of middle America; the wilds of Appalachia; the wastelands of the inner cities; it's the community next door; it's the developing nations abroad. It is past time to do this thing—to do what Jesus called us to do when he said, "Whatever you do to the least of these, you're also doing it to me" (see Matthew 25:40).

Whatever you do for our honored guests from the Gulf Coast states (maybe of who are still among us) or for anyone who is down and out, you are doing the same thing for God. Be generous. Be kind. Reach out—and do the doggone thing!

12. Refuse to Be a Victim

I think all of us know that life can really make a victim out of you. Have you ever felt like you were a victim—that life was down on you and as a consequence you became down on yourself? That's what happens when you become a victim. What goes wrong around you gets inside you, sabotaging your spirit, messing with your mind, and causing you to conclude there is no way possible that anything will change, that anything will ever get better.

Have you ever felt like a victim because of what has happened to you? Have you ever felt like a victim because things were not going right for you? Well, I've got some wonderful news. I was reading the newspaper the other day and it blew me away.[1] There's a bad sister by the name of Charlotte Johnson over in Fort Worth. This young woman in Tarrant County was taking her daughter to school when they stopped off at McDonalds shortly after 8:00 in the morning. Suddenly this man got out in front of Charlotte and had the nerve to come out of his trunk with a bat! It was the wrong thing to do with the wrong woman. Her teenage daughter was dialing 911, but Charlotte knew the police would not get there on time. What did she do? She refused to be a victim, and home girl got the upper hand. Mr. Bat Man was carried off with a busted head, and I'll bet you he won't mess with Charlotte Johnson again!

Reading that news story, I realized that there are all kinds of things that go wrong in our lives. People come at us in the wrong way. But you can refuse to go out like that. You can have the mentality that in Christ you are not a victim but a victor.

What does that mean? First, don't ever *allow* yourself to be a victim. How? Simply by recognizing that every now and then you have to take things into your own hands. That's why I believe that the best helping hand you will ever find is at the end of your own arm. Let me say that again because it is good. *The best helping hand you will ever find is at the end of your own arm.*

That's what Charlotte realized. Since help wouldn't arrive in time, Charlotte decided to take things into her own hands. You can't always wait for somebody else to do something for you. Sometimes you have to step up yourself and say, "Hey! I'm responsible. I'm grown. I'm going to take things into my own hands."

...sometimes you need to open up the Word of God and take what I call your "anti-victim vitamins."

Second, when life comes at you wrong, realize that you have a power within you that comes from God and will help you defeat anything that comes at you. Sometimes you need to open up the Word of God and take what I call your "anti-victim vitamins."

What are anti-victim vitamins? Well, one is vitamin A: "And we know that all things work together for good to them that love God, to them who are called according to his purpose" (Romans 8:28, KJV). Vitamin C is "Cast all your cares on God, knowing God cares for you" (see 1 Peter 5:7). Don't forget vitamin T: "The LORD is my light and my salvation; whom shall I fear? The Lord is the stronghold of my life; of whom shall I be afraid?" (Psalm 27:1, NRSV). I hope there's somebody out there who says, "Yes, life may go wrong, *but I refuse to be a victim*!"

Note
1. James Ragland, "Drive-Through Defense: Threatened Outside Eatery, Woman Refused to Be a Victim." *Dallas Morning News,* March 9, 2006.

13. It Hurts but You Will Heal

Life hurts. If you have lived very long at all, you will agree with that statement. This painful reality hits all of us. I don't care who you are, sooner or later you are going to collide with the fact that life does hurt. Your heart will be broken. Your spirit will find itself almost shattered to the point where you don't feel like going on. Sometimes life hurts so much it's hard to get up in the morning. That's why I like to quote African American poet Paul Laurence Dunbar, who wrote the poem entitled simply "Life":

A crust of bread and a corner to sleep in,
A minute to smile and an hour to weep in,
A pint of joy to a peck of trouble,

And never a laugh but the moans come double;
And that is life![1]

Why? Because life hurts. Even now, you may be experiencing firsthand the pain that life can bring. I don't know why you are in pain, but you are in pain and you know life hurts.

In the weekend edition of *USA Today*, there was a special front page feature on head coach Tony Dungy of the Indianapolis Colts football team.[2] Coach Dungy has known pain at its greatest level. Why? Because on December 2, 2005, his eighteen-year-old son took his own life. How heartbreaking! As a parent in that situation, you feel helpless. You feel guilty. You feel enraged. You feel the question: Why? Why? Why? Well, that's what Tony Dungy has been asking himself in the long months since his son's death. But Dungy inspired me in that article because he also said he has discovered that pain is a part of the healing process.

I want to pass on the lessons from Tony Dungy because he teaches us that even when life hurts and you feel like you've come to a dead end, God is setting you up for a brand-new beginning. I know it hurts, but you *will* heal.

Lesson #1: Learn to *ex*press how you feel and don't *re*press it, or you will get *de*pressed. Why? Because if you hold in your emotions and pain and try to be hard and play like you do not need to talk about it, the hurt will become cancerous. It will get inside you and poison you.

**Learn to *ex*press how you feel and don't *re*press it,
or you will get *de*pressed.**

What you want to do is release your pain by expressing how you feel in a context of healing and nonjudgment. Please *express* it; don't *repress* it.

Lesson #2: Make sure you take some time for yourself to heal. It's all right to call time out from life or to say you need to get away and spend some time with yourself and God.

Lesson #3: You will heal if you turn *to* God and not *from* God. We sing a wonderful song in church by Richard Smallwood called "Healing." It is a word of encouragement in sickness and sorrow. It is a reminder that joy returns in the morning—and that God is always nearby. There is a Balm in Gilead, intended for the healing of your soul.

That's the good news of the day. I know life hurts, but you *will* heal. And when you do heal, you will emerge stronger than you were before you were hurt. Thank God for Tony Dungee who stands as a witness to declare: I know it hurts, but you will heal.

Notes
1. Paul Laurence Dunbar, "Life," http://www.dunbarsite.org/gallery/Life.asp (accessed March 26, 2007).
2. http://www.usatoday.com/sports/football/nfl/colts/2005-12-22-dungy-son_x.htm (accessed May 3, 2007).

14. What Are You Doing to Carry On the Legacy?

This reflection is based on a radio message delivered the day that Coretta Scott King passed away. It is a tribute to that great woman.

We all know life can be hard and unfair. There is so much pain to endure, heartbreak to heal, obstacles to overcome, nightmares to dispel from disrupting our dreams. But imagine this. Imagine that after two years of marriage you begin living every day under the threat of violent death. Imagine living a life in which your life is no longer *your* life. Imagine thirteen years of living with that threat of violence, knowing your husband may be killed or taken from you. Then imagine that fifteen years into your marriage, the news finally comes, and of course it's all over. Your husband is dead—killed by an assassin's bullet. Imagine living that kind of life.

Well, that's exactly what Coretta Scott King endured, and of course, on January 30, 2006, we learned of her passing. It was sad news, but I considered her life and all that she endured with amazing grace and stalwart dignity. I considered her life and realized that some thirty-eight years after her husband was tragically killed, she continued to carry the legacy of Martin Luther King Jr. She continued to make his dream a reality, even in the face of the most painful and harsh nightmares that life had to offer.

Remembering Coretta Scott King's life and how she carried on her martyred husband's work, I raise the question of legacy. My question is what are *you* doing with legacy that Dr. King and so many others have bequeathed us? Do you not know it's a slap in the face of that legacy whenever we bow to racism, conform to evil, refuse to take a stand against injustice, sell out with drugs, and find ourselves partying—when we *should* be planning and handling our own business?

I want to know today what you are doing with the legacy that has been left to you. I lift up Coretta Scott King as a shining example of what it means in the face of nightmares to handle your business and to make sure that you carry on the legacy to fulfill the dream that God has for all of us—a dream that was embodied in the life and legacy of the late great Dr. Martin Luther King Jr.

I thank God for Coretta Scott King because her life

Your faith *only* works when it is a faith that works.

teaches me at least three lessons that I will pass on to you. First, she teaches us to have the resilience to bounce back even when life knocks us down. Think about how she endured so much, went through so much, and yet she kept on bouncing back. Bouncing back after her husband was killed. Bouncing back after her home was bombed in Montgomery, Alabama. No matter how hard life got or unfair it was to her, with grace and dignity, she kept bouncing back. That is what it will take if you are going to live up to a legacy. Life is going to get you down and people will try to knock you down, but you make up your mind and declare, "I'm going to bounce back."

Second, when your worst nightmare gives you every excuse to be down, resolve to stand up and fulfill the dream. That's what Coretta Scott King did. On April 4, 1968, her husband was killed. She got the word, and she planned the funeral. Then after the funeral, she stood up and went to Memphis, Tennessee, where Doc had been killed, and there she led the striking sanitation workers' march. That's what it means to hold up the legacy. That's what it means to stand up in the face of your worst nightmare and still be true to your highest dream.

That's what I'm saying to you. You've endured a horrible nightmarish situation and you have every excuse to give up, but when others expect you to give up, that's when you stand up and step up and remain true to your dream.

Finally, Coretta King teaches me that *your faith only works when it is a faith that works.* I love that. Let me do that again. Your faith *only* works when it is a faith that works. This woman of faith fought for human rights, social justice, and world peace while continuing to raise four remarkable children as a single parent. That's what I call a faith that works. Never forget that your faith only works when it is a faith that works.

Yes, we love Dr. Martin Luther King; yes, we commemorate the life of Coretta Scott King; but the question of today is *what are you doing to carry on the legacy?*

15. I'm Lovin' It

I was really blessed recently while talking to Damon Wayans. The first thing I asked him was, "How're you doin'?" His response was simply, "Hey, I'm just loving life." And I'm loving that answer because too many people cannot say that. They move through life with a nasty disposition. They have a pessimistic perspective on everything that goes wrong. They see the glass half *empty* as opposed to half *full*. They are not loving life. They are simply going through the motions in life. My question is: Are you going through the motions today, or can you say with Damon Wayans, "I'm loving this life"?

Let me see if I can make this plain. A little boy was placed in a room with nothing but manure. Have you ever felt like that? That you were in a stinky mess in terms of

**Happiness is something you find within yourself....
If you aren't happy with you, you aren't going to be
happy with anybody else....**

the situation you were in? They left the boy in there, and
then they came back about an hour later. The boy was
covered in manure, and he was digging through the stuff,
putting it in piles around him. Bewildered, they asked the
boy, "What are you doing?" He replied, "There has to be
a pony in here somewhere with all of this manure."

That little boy was placed in a stinky situation, but he
loved life and had such a positive outlook that he was
looking for something positive in the midst of all that was
negative. That's my word of the day. In the midst of whatever
may be nasty, stinky, and bad in your life, can you find
the kind of positive outlook that says, "I'm loving life"?

Basically, "I'm loving life" says three things. First, it says,
"Even when hate comes my way, because of my love for
life, I'm not going to allow that hate to bring me down to
your level." You *will* have haters in this life, but when you
are loving life, you won't allow their hatred to get into
your system and bring you down on their level.

Second, when you love life, you find that happiness is
not something you find in a place or a person. Happiness
is something you find within yourself. It's not something
you find by dating this person or moving to this place. In
a real sense your happiness comes from within. If you

aren't happy with you, you aren't going to be happy with anybody else or in any other place.

Finally, when you are loving life, it's because you recognize that God has given you a gift called life and what you do with that life is *your gift back to God*. I like that. I read that idea somewhere. It said something like, "Everything you have is God's gift to you; what you do with it is your gift back to God."

I'm like Damon Wayans. I know life can be rough, but the bottom line is I've made up my mind. I'm *loving* this life.

16. Handling Your Hurricane

In 2005 we were all praying for those who experienced the horrors of the hurricanes along the Gulf Coast. Katrina and Rita destroyed lives and property—and many people and places are still struggling to recover. Yet you don't have to live on the Gulf to have experienced hurricane-like devastation. Every now and then, life catches us up in a hurricane of troubles, a hurricane of difficulties—and a hurricane of any kind can be disruptive. Hurricanes can leave you "tore up from the floor up" and wondering even if you'll ever be able to get up.

Today you may be going through your own personal hurricane. Maybe you're laid off from your job. Maybe there's hell in your home. Maybe you're battered by illness. All of us know something about personal hurricanes. The

How might the hurricane be used by God to develop you instead of destroying you?

question is, when you're going through a hurricane, how might the hurricane be used by God to develop you instead of destroying you?

Ralph Douglas West, my friend and brother pastor in Houston, Texas, talked about a friend of his who owns a boat. The friend told Pastor West that whenever there is a hurricane or a storm, he doesn't keep his boat at the dock. Instead, he takes the boat out into the deep water. Once the boat is out deep, he lets the anchor down because the anchor keeps the boat from drifting away. He says the boat belongs in a storm, and if you don't want to lose the boat, make sure you anchor it deeply.

I thought about that. Boats belong in the storm. Boats can handle the storm. But if you don't want to lose the boat, you've got to anchor deeply. That's what I'm suggesting to you. If you're going through a hurricane right now, make sure you anchor deeply. How do you do that? I'll give you two strategies for anchoring your spirit in deep waters.

1. Use the best anchor there is, and that's called prayer. If you learn how to pray, God has a way of being your anchor in the storm. And there is no better starting place for prayer than what Jesus taught the disciples: "Our

Father which art in heaven, hallowed be thy name...."

2. The second anchor is called faith. It's one thing to pray; it's another to believe that God is able to hear your prayers and act on them. So that's another anchor that you can use in a storm.

There is a hymn called "My Soul Has Been Anchored in the Lord." That's how to handle your hurricane. Make sure you go out in deep water, and then make sure you anchor deeply in faith-filled prayer.

17. Good *to* Us and Good *through* Us

We are often quick to say how good God is. People say, "God is good to me. I'm blessed and highly favored. God woke me up this morning and started me on my way." We can talk about how good God is, yet if God doesn't let a job come through, doesn't let a new car come to us, doesn't let a house become available to us, then will we still be shouting all over the place about how good God is? Let me tell you something: God is good *to* us in order to be good *through* us. Simply put, unless the blessing that God has given *to* you gets *through* you, it will become a curse *on* you.

Many of you know people who have a whole lot of stuff. They have a king-size bed, but they can't get a good night's sleep. They have a luxury car, but they have no sense of direction. They can't seem to enjoy their blessings. Why? Because the blessing got *to* them, but it didn't get *through* them.

In the last five or ten years, we have faced some major trials in this country: the terrorist attacks of September 11, 2001, the hurricanes of recent years (especially Katrina in 2005), the escalating violence in cities and suburbs alike. But I'm thinking about how good God has been to us through it all. And if you want God to continue to be good to you, then remember: God gives blessings *to* you so God can get blessings *through* you. In other words, God wants to be good *to* you in order to do good *through* you—because the blessings you receive aren't just about you. If they stop at you, then sadly, those blessings will become a curse.

So instead of talking about how good God is *to* us, let's talk about how good God is *through* us. How does God want to be good through us? First, take a look at what God has done for us. We often talk about how God in grace has given us a fresh start, another chance. We've blown it and yet God has given us the opportunity to start over. Isn't that what those who have been victimized need? Survivors of violence, tragedy, hurricanes, or any other circumstance—they need a fresh start. That's something you can do. You can appreciate your blessing of a fresh start by *being* a blessing to those who also need a fresh start.

Second, God not only blesses us with things that money *can* buy, but also with things that money *can't* buy. One of

God is good *to* us in order to be good *through* us.

those blessings is time. You can't put a price tag on the time you give, and there are so many things you can do for people who have been victimized. God gives blessings to you in order to get blessings through you. You can give your time to volunteer to help the survivors of this life.

Finally, think about every blessing you have received. Let's call them your "hook-ups" from God. So if God has hooked you up, then you use your hook-up to hook somebody else up. Think about how good God has been to you; then go out and be good to somebody else. We are, after all, one family in the eyes of God. God has been good *to* us; now let's allow God to be good *through* us.

18. Time to Break the Cycle

Do you ever feel as if, in spite of your highest efforts and greatest wishes, you keep ending up in the same old place? You know what a cycle is, don't you? A cycle is when you start well, you have good intentions, but somehow you make a wrong turn and end up where you did not want to end up. As a consequence you keep going where you've gone, doing what you've done. It's a never-ending and even vicious pattern of the same old thing, whereby you end up in the same old place.

It's kind of like the story I heard about these men who had gone to a party. The party was across the lake from where they lived, so they had used a rowboat to get to the party. Late that night, after the party was over, they got in the rowboat to return home. It was late at night or really

Doing what you have been doing means you are going to go where you've always gone and get what you've always gotten.

early in the morning, so the sky was pitch black. But it was only a short distance across the lake, and they knew the way, so they got in the rowboat and started rowing. They rowed and rowed and kept rowing, and they couldn't figure out why they never seemed to arrive on the opposite shore. Well, when morning finally dawned, they realized that in their drunken stupor, they had been rowing around in circles. Why? Because they had forgotten to raise the anchor tied to the boat, and naturally, the anchor had kept them from making any progress.

Watch this. They kept going where they had gone, doing what they had done. Why? Because no one had taken the time to pull up the anchor. In a real sense, if you're not careful, you'll keep doing the same old thing, ending up in the same old place. You can change people in your life and you can change jobs, but—watch this—you will end up in the same old place. Why? Because you haven't pulled up whatever anchor has you stuck in a never-ending cycle.

How do you break the cycle? I'm glad you asked! Step one: You break the cycle when you recognize the pattern—when you realize that doing what you have been doing means you are going to go where you've always gone and get what you've always gotten. You have to recognize the pattern and choose to change it. You have to change your mind. You have to change some basic things about the way you think and act and react. Once you change internally, then things can change for you externally.

Step two: You break the cycle when you recognize that God gives you the power to break the cycle. How does God empower you to break the cycle? I'll give it to you like this. Not long ago I had a very important meeting in Washington, DC. I was on the plane, and the plane got in a holding pattern waiting to land. Finally, after thirty minutes of circling the DC area, the pilot announced over the intercom, "I've just received clearance from the control tower. Now we can land." We had been circling the skies above the DC area, stuck in a holding pattern, in a cycle as it were, but the pilot said, "The control tower has just given us clearance to land."

That's my word to you today. God is in the control tower, and God says you don't have to stay in that holding pattern. You don't have to stay in the same old cycle. You've been given clearance to land. Jesus put it this way: "You will know the truth, and the truth will make you free" (John 8:32, NRSV). You've been given clearance to land. And if God has set you free, you are free indeed.

That's the word of the day. You don't have to stay in the same old cycle doing what you've done and going where you've gone. God gives you power to break the cycle—first by changing your mind and then by changing your situation. It's time to break that cycle!

19. Signs of Hope When Your World Is Torn Up

It's hard to dream when you've been living a nightmare. It's tough to look up when life has knocked you down. Sometimes it hurts too much to pray. Even though you believe God is a heart fixer, sometimes you just hurt too much to pray.

Sometimes you feel so bad you have a hard time believing that God is still good. Yet I'm convinced that if you hold on to hope, you are somehow able to keep your faith alive. In your heart you will find that hope believes in the future despite the darkness of the present and the hurts of the past. In fact, the difference between a survivor and a victim is most often that spirit of hope—hope that struggles to stay alive even when the world is torn up all around you.

The year 2005 was a record-breaking year for tropical storms and hurricanes in the Atlantic and Gulf of Mexico. More and worse storms hit the islands and mainland alike, and the stories and photos that emerged from those storms were stunning in their devastation and tragedy. Florida was particularly hard hit by a series of hurricanes, one of which destroyed much of central Florida.

But do you know what? While I was checking out pictures of that area in the aftermath of the storms, I discovered one photo of a flower in the midst of the debris left by that terrible hurricane. There was a flower growing out of the debris. It was a powerful picture. Can you see on the screen of your anointed imagination a flower growing out of the rubble left by a hurricane? All around it there was nothing but devastation, and yet that flower rose above it all.

Isn't that flower a sign of hope? That's the way our God works. In a situation where everything is torn up from the floor up, God will send signs of hope. What does that mean? One, it means that God can use the devastation to bring out of us what God has put in us. Perhaps that flower never would have blossomed had that hurricane not come through that area in central Florida. The flower testifies that what happened to it somehow brought out what God had put in it.

Two, the flower lets us know that sometimes you have to go through a whole lot of dirt before you can blossom. In fact, a farmer will tell you the value of the foulest fertilizer

Sometimes you feel so bad you have a hard time believing that God is still good.

when it comes to making things grow! You'll go through a lot of dirt before you blossom. That's my word to you today. I know it looks dark sometimes. I know it hurts sometimes. But keep your eyes open and your spirit in tune. God has a way of giving us hope even when our world is torn up.

20. To Play the Game, You Have to Change the Game

If you don't know who you are—guess what—other folks will be more than happy to tell you. Don't you get tired of people putting you in a box and trying to get you to live *down* to their expectations? They try to define you. Whenever you allow others to *de*fine you, they can *con*fine you. So make sure you play your own game even if you have to change the game.

Recently I heard a powerful interview with Kanye West on the radio. He's one bad brother. During the interview he said, "I'm out to change the game." Kanye West dared to challenge the status quo while keeping it real with himself. And guess what? That is what life is all about. Sometimes you've got to change the game if you're going to play your game.

Why? Because people are quick to *define* you so they can *confine* you. People are quick to put you in a box and tell you what you can or cannot do based on their definition of you. But recognize the wisdom of Kanye West who was out to change the game. One poet put it like this:

> Many a somebody who fell in line became a nobody in almost no time;
> Anyone can follow what the crowds do, but I'm somebody—how about you?
> Everybody's doing it. No, not yet. I'm somebody. Don't you forget.
> Anyone with courage to see what's true is bound to be somebody—
> How about you?

In other words, you have to play your game and sometimes that means you have to *change* the game. And that brings me to the three things I have to pass on to you today.

1. Define yourself for yourself so you won't be someone other than yourself.

2. When you define yourself, don't forget that God made you uniquely you. Don't settle for anything less than the you God made.

3. Learn to be a thermo*stat* not a thermo*meter*. A thermometer just registers and records the temperature, but a thermostat regulates and controls the temperature. So

**Any time you allow someone else to *def*ine you,
they can *con*fine you.**

make up your mind to change the game by playing your own game. Be a thermostat and not a thermometer.

I'm with Kanye West. I'm going to play my game even if I have to change the game. Paul put it this way in Romans 12:2, "Do not be conformed to this world, but be transformed by the renewing of your minds" (NRSV).

21. Think Like a Champion

If you're going to get in it, why don't you think you can win it? Start thinking like a champion! That's the word of the day: *Think like a champion*. Why? Because sadly, most people go through life not expecting much. They don't want much. They don't do much. As a consequence, that's exactly what they get out of life: not much. You know them because—watch this—they go around thinking *down*. You think *up*; they try to pull you down to their level. Too many people in life are just mired in mediocrity. They don't want much out of life. They ain't going to do much. They don't want to be much.

That's a sad situation. Why? God did not make you to be a not-much person. God made you to be a champion. You have to give major props to our boy Avery Johnson, coach of the Dallas Mavericks, who was deservedly named 2005–2006 NBA Coach of the Year. What I love so much about Coach Johnson is that he has brought a new mind-set to the Mavericks. Before Johnson came on the scene, the team was content to make the playoffs. Now they're thinking about winning it all because Johnson's mentality is "If you're going to be in it, you might as well win it."

Don't you love that? In a real sense, *that* is the mentality of a champion. My question is what is your mentality? Because your mind will take you down or your mind will take you up. That's why a poet said,

> If you think you're beaten, you are;
>   if you think you dare not, you don't.
> If you like to win but you think you can't,
>   it's almost a cinch you won't.
> If you think you're outclassed, you are.
> You've got to think high to ride.
> You've got to be sure of yourself
>   if you want to win the prize.
> Life's battles don't always go
>   to the stronger or faster man,
> But sooner or later the man who wins
>   is the one who thinks he can.

Avery Johnson thinks he can, and because *he* thinks he can, the Mavericks have started to believe *they* can. My

It is not your personality but your mentality that will shape your reality.

question today is, what is your mentality? Is it that of a champ or of a chump?

Well, what do we learn from Coach Johnson? Two lessons to start you on your way today. First—and please don't miss this—in this life, *it is not your personality but your mentality that will shape your reality.* I like that. What's on your mind will shape the world you shape for yourself. So, it is not your personality but your mentality that will shape your reality.

Second, if you will allow God to get in your head, then God will cause you to think God-sized thoughts. When God is in your head, you have the power to move ahead. I'm with Coach Johnson. If you're going to be in it, why don't you make sure that you win it. That's why I love Paul when he says, "I press on toward the goal for the prize of the heavenly call of God in Christ Jesus" (Philippians 3:14, NRSV). Or as Eugene Peterson's *The Message* puts it, "I'm off and running, and I'm not turning back."

In other words, don't have the mentality of a chump. Have the mentality of a champ! Like Avery Johnson, Paul teaches us to have the mind-set of a champion.

22. When Things Get Out of Hand

You know life can go real wrong real fast. You can be up today and down tonight. That's why you shouldn't get up on your high horse and look down at other people when you're up. Tomorrow or even later today, your positions could be reversed!

Every now and then it seems life is spinning totally out of control and you feel handcuffed by helplessness to do anything to change or conquer the circumstances in which you find yourself. And so the question is, what do you do when there is nothing you *can* do? Life has gotten out of hand. What do you do when you don't know what to do? Every now and then you reach a point in your life where you throw up your hands in frustration. Life has gotten completely out of control.

I don't know *how*, but I do know *who*.

A while back my aunt Serita was in the hospital. She had received a negative diagnosis, and many of us were praying for her. I was speaking with her and she blessed me when she said, "Hey, don't trip. Just put it in God's hands because God's hands can handle it. But don't try to take it back out of God's hands once you place it in God's hands." And then she quoted that old song we used to sing in church: "Take your burden to the Lord and leave it there. If you trust and never doubt, He will surely bring you out. Take your burden to the Lord and leave it there."[1]

Her words blessed me, because it dawned on me that every now and then, each of us doesn't know what to do when things get out of hand. The song says, "Take your burden to the Lord and leave it there." When it's out of your hands, it's in God's hands.

Let me remind you what this means. One, it means do what you can and then trust God to handle what you can't. Basically all you can do is do what you can—and then trust that God is going to do what you can't.

Two, hang in there and trust that God is going to come through somehow. You can say, "I don't know *how*, but I do know *who*." I don't know *how* this door is going to open, but I do know *who* is a door opener. I don't know *how* I'm going to get through, but I do know *who* is going to carry me through. I don't know *how* I'm going to deal with those who hate me, but I do know *who* is going to prepare a table before me in the presence of my enemies. I don't know *how*, but I do know *who*.

When things get out of hand, take them and place them in God's hands. Take your burdens to the Lord and leave them there.

Note
1. "Leave It There," words and music by Charles A. Tindley, 1916.

23. Serving Your Way to the Top

There are people who think they can scheme, backstab, and connive their way up the ladder of success. They always have a scheme. They always have a plan. Sometimes they will use the knives they put in your back as rungs to climb up the ladder of success. But this isn't the way to go. In life there is such a thing as the principle of reaping what you sow, of what goes around comes around. If you want to reach the top, the way to make life better for *you* is for *you* to make life better for *others*. Why? Because whenever you make life better for somebody else, it always boomerangs back to you.

Mohammad Yunus, a businessman from Bangladesh, was awarded the Nobel Peace Prize in 2006. Yunus is convinced that the way to bring peace to the world is by eradicating poverty. So Yunus makes loans to people who are impoverished. As a consequence of his conviction, today in Bangladesh you have people who used to be poor who are now operating their own businesses. Yunus loaned them the necessary money to escape their poverty, and in doing so, he was able to serve his way to the top.

A few years ago I was in Africa staying in a hotel, and my room was on the top floor. The sister who was trying to show me the way said, "The only way to reach the top, where your room is, is to take the service elevator." I had to take a service elevator to my room because no other elevator was working. That's what Muhammad Yunus has done. He has recognized that in this life if you want to reach the top, you have to take the service elevator. That's what's going to take you up. You don't have to connive; you don't have to scheme; you don't have to stab anybody in the back. The way to reach the top is through service.

What does that mean? First, it's not about how much you are doing, but how much you're doing for other people. You'll discover there is no real fulfillment in life like the fulfillment of knowing you are touching somebody else's life, that you are being a blessing to somebody.

Second, it's not about making a better place in the world; it's about you making this world a better place for others. Make up your mind to say, "I'm not just going to make myself a better place in the world, but I'm going to do all I can to make this world a better place for everyone."

If you want to reach the top, the way to make life better for _you_ is for _you_ to make life better for _others_.

I have discovered that in this life the real test of your service is what you are doing for people who will never be able to pay you back. Are you a voice for those who are voiceless? Are you helping those who are helpless? What are you doing for those who are homeless? What are you doing for those children who have an absentee parent? The real test of your service is what you are doing for those who will never be able to pay you back. You have to keep that cycle of blessings going.

If you want to reach the top, please make sure you do it through service.

24. Turning Things Around

Have you ever felt as if things in your life just weren't going the way you wanted them to go? Have you ever had one of those days when you started off on the wrong foot, and it seemed like no matter what you tried to do that, you just couldn't correct things? Each one of us has had those bad starts to begin a year, to begin a relationship, to begin a career. We want to get off on the right foot, but wrong just dogs our footsteps and we find ourselves saying, "How did I get where I am?"

The good news is that you can turn things around. Not long ago I ran into a friend of mine from high school, and this brother had been super bad in basketball in high school. He was awesome—but seeing him made me flashback to one game. In the first half, this superstar had nothing but

**You see, before you can quit it,
you've got to admit it.**

bricks. You could have built the American Airlines Center with his brick shots. He just wasn't having a good game. The first half he was zero for twelve.

When we ran into each other recently, I asked my friend about that game, and he told me that at halftime, the coach had pulled him aside. The coach said to him, "Here's what you need to do. You need to make this adjustment right here. Make this correction on your shot." Then the coach said, "I want you to start the second half."

Now, my friend had just known he was going to be benched after blowing the first half. However, the coach gave him some halftime adjustments and then told him, "You're starting in the third quarter." And guess what. The boy went out and threw down! In fact, he hit the game-winning shot on a play the coach had designed just for him. In spite of a sorry, jacked-up first half, my friend was able to come through big-time in the second half. How? Because the coach gave him the power to turn things around.

I am talking to somebody. I don't know who you are, but you feel like your life has gotten off track. Things aren't going the way you want them to. Here's the good news: the Coach of the Cosmos believes in you. God will give you the power to turn things around.

How do you turn things around? First, you can't get things right until you admit what has gone wrong. You see, before you can quit it, you've got to admit it. My friend had to admit to the jacked-up first half before he could accept the coach's correction and excel in the second half. Only when you see where you are wrong are you able to make the right choice.

Second, remember that you can *choose* to change. You don't have to stay where you are. Nobody can keep you there—unless you give that person the permission to do so. That's why the British poet John Oxenham wrote,

> To every man there openeth A way, and ways, and a way. And the high soul climbs the high way, And the low soul gropes the low: And in between, on the misty flats, The rest drift to and fro. But to every man there openeth A high way and a low, And every man decideth. The way his soul shall go.[1]

You can turn things around *if* you remember you have the power of choice. You can *choose* to *change*. And once you change your mind, you can change your life.

Third and finally, you can turn things around because the Coach gives us another chance. God is another-chance God. Every single minute, every single hour, every single day, God is saying, "Here's another chance." Here's another chance to undo what was done. Here's another chance to make your life what it should be. Here's another chance to choose to do right even though you may have gone wrong. God is the God of another chance. In faith we call that *grace*—amazing grace that has a wonderful way of looking beyond our faults, seeing our needs, and helping us to turn things around.

Note
1. http://www.quotationsbook.com/author/5510/ (accessed March 28, 2007).

25. What Are You Doing Here?

This question gives me a horrible flashback to one of my earliest memories. When I was little, my father sent me to his office to get a magazine. I got sidetracked once I got there because in my father's office was a pool table. It was a nice pool table and I thought I was a pool shark. And so, although I had been sent to get his magazine, I ended up spending time at the pool table. Time went by. Next thing I knew, I heard the booming baritone of my father's voice, "What are you doing here? I sent you for a magazine. What are you doing here?" Naturally, my childish response was "I don't know." I was guilty of not doing what I was sent there to do.

Then my father, who was old school when it came to discipline, began to whip me and talk to me at the same

When you know *what* your *why* is, then trust God to handle the *how*.

time. *Pow*! "Make sure you do know..." *Pow*! "Make sure you do know why you are here." And that lesson has stayed with me all my life.

My question to you right now is, what are you doing here? God our heavenly Father is asking that question too. Are you doing what you're supposed to be doing? Are you doing what you've been sent to do? What are you doing here?

I've been reading a book called *Born to Preach: Essays in Honor of Henry and Ella Mitchell*.[1] The thematic thread of the essays is that both of the Mitchells have discovered what they were born to do and what they were meant to do. They *know* what they are doing here. Who *wouldn't* want to be like the Mitchells when we "grow up"?

If you know what you're doing here, there are three blessings you'll recognize. One, when you know what you're doing here, you develop an allergic reaction to settling for settling. You won't get distracted and you won't settle for something less than the best that God has for you. When I was sent for a magazine and ended up playing pool, I settled for settling.

Two, to find what you've been sent for, check with the One who sent you. God placed each of us on this planet for a purpose. There is no aimless life. There is no purposeless life. You must check with the One who sent you.

Finally, once you know why you've been sent here, you can trust God to handle the *how* of accomplishing your purpose. Let me rephrase that: When you know *what* your *why* is, then trust God to handle the *how*. Don't ask, "How am I going to get this done? How is this door going to open?" Your responsibility is to know *what* you're doing here. It's God's responsibility to handle the *how*.

The question for today is, what you doing here?

Note
1. Samuel K. Roberts, ed., *Born to Preach: Essays in Honor of Henry and Ella Mitchell* (Valley Forge, PA: Judson Press, 2000).

26. We Belong Together

"We belong together." That's what Mariah Carey says in her popular song by the same name. We belong together. But today I want to look at that insight from a different perspective—because I've discovered that divide and conquer is an old trick. It's a tried and true trick. It's an effective trick. We belong together, but divide and conquer always works.

I came across an African parable about these small birds that were fighting over one worm. And while they were fighting over this one worm, a bigger bird swooped down and took the worm they were fighting over. Divide and conquer is tried and true because it always works.

Have you heard the story about the quail that were trapped by the bird hunter? The quail were trapped under

When we pull together instead of pulling apart, we can make a difference.

this net, and they began fighting each other, saying, "If it hadn't been for you, I wouldn't be trapped under this net"—each blaming the others. But then one of them said, "We've got the power! Let's flap our wings together." And when they began to flap their wings in synchronization, they had enough power to lift that which had trapped them. And they were able to go free. Why? Because they had recognized that they belonged together.

When we pull together instead of pulling apart, we can make a difference. When you have new neighbors, whether they have come as survivors of a disaster such as Hurricane Katrina or they just joined your church or moved into your neighborhood, treat them in a way that's warm and wonderful, because, in the final analysis, we belong together.

What does that mean? What are the implications of that statement? Let me break it down into three simple truths.

1. As Martin Luther King Jr. put it so succinctly, "If we don't learn to hang together, then we'll hang one by one."

2. Whenever you bless somebody else, that blessing will boomerang back to you. What goes around has a way of coming around.

3. When you understand that we belong together, you will recognize what God has for you. Nobody can take *from* you what God has *for* you.

Free yourself from comparing yourself with other people and competing for their possessions. Be a blessing to somebody else and see how that blessing comes back around to you. Remember, *we belong together*.

27. You Really Are All Right

I came across something that really hurt me the other day. It was a suicide note left by someone who wrote, "My life is worth nothing. I feel like a peanut in Yankee Stadium; therefore, I'm going to go ahead and crush myself and get rid of myself." This person was obviously depressed.

Too many people waste their lives comparing and competing with others and trying to be something or someone they are not. When they compare themselves to somebody else, they feel like mere peanuts in Yankee Stadium. When you spend your life competing and comparing yourself, you are engaging in what I call self-rejection, the worst rejection of all is when you don't accept you for who you are and for who God made you, then you are engaging in self-rejection.

**Whenever you try to be a copy of somebody else,
you're second best, at best.**

One of my favorite movies is Eddie Murphy's remake of *The Nutty Professor*. Sherman Clump, the professor, is in love with the lovely Ms. Purty, but because he is so overweight, he feels he isn't worthy of her. So instead of being himself, he tries to shortcut success by taking a potion to become someone else—a smooth, skinny guy named Buddy Love. The potion Sherman had taken to get skinny wears off, and at the end of this disaster, he has to explain himself in front of everyone at a big party. He says to the assembled crowd, "I guess I need to accept me for who I am."

That's a heavy lesson. *I need to accept me for who I am.* I really am all right just the way I am. And if you can't accept me for who I am, that's not *my* problem; it's *your* problem. See, we really are all right. All of us, just as we are created.

What does that mean for you today? I'm going to quote the classic: "Be what you is and not what you ain't. Cause if you ain't what you is, you is what you ain't." Hambone is saying be who you are and quit trying to be a carbon copy of somebody else. Because whenever you try to be a copy of somebody else, you're second best, at best.

Next, when you accept you, you'll quit trippin' on what others think of you. You'll be free to be the "you" that

God made you to be. Learn to be the best you that God made. You really are all right the way you are.

Finally, look at all that God has done for you, and you'll know that you really are something special. You really are all right! God has sustained you through all you have experienced. God has blessed you with what you have. Evidently God has something special in store for you.

You see, the Bible refers to us as God's workmanship (Ephesians 2:10). I like the New Living Translation, which declares "we are God's masterpiece." Yes, I am a masterpiece—God's masterpiece. And so are you. We really are all right. I'm with Sherman Clump. I'm going to have to start accepting me for who I am.

28. A Love That Is Unpredictable

Too many people are what I call repeat offenders in life. They keep making the same old bad choices, getting the same old bad consequences. Hey, if you do what you have always done, you are going to get what you've always got. It's logical, but these repeat offenders wonder why: "Why do I keep on getting in these same old stupid situations?" They are repeat offenders.

Others live what I call rerun lives. You know what a rerun is on television. You see the same old show with the same old characters with the same old plot. Well, for a lot of us, if we are not careful, every day can become a rerun. Nothing different! Just the same!

Not long ago our home boy Jamie Foxx was tearing up the chart with his hot hit "Unpredictable." "It's off the hizzle for shizzle," Snoop Dog would say. The message is heavy. He's saying, why settle for the usual when you can experience the unpredictable? You can experience something that is off the chain, something totally unexpected and surprising. In a real sense, Foxx is saying life should be adventurous. All this ain't no dress rehearsal. So why settle for the usual? Why settle for being a repeat offender? Why settle for a life of nothing but reruns?

Your life, my friend, needs to be unpredictable. How can that happen? I promise you it will work—if you experience what is means to be loved by God. OK, so maybe on Valentine's Day nobody sent you flowers, but hey, God loves you so much he sent you the Lily of the Valley. God loves you so much he offers you the Bright and Morning Star. I am trying to give it to you like this: You really haven't been loved 'til God loves you, and when God loves you, life is going to be unpredictable.

Unpredictable how? In three ways. First, when God loves you in God's unpredictable way, you can count on the fact that God's love is *unconditional.* Don't you love that? You see, God's love isn't sometime-y or determined by what you can do for God. God loves you whether you like it or not. If you make a mistake, God still loves you. If you blow it, God still loves you. If you don't do the right thing, God still loves you. You haven't been loved until you've been loved by God.

Second, God's love is *healing.* How many of us have been torn up from the floor up? Felt like we could not get

You haven't been loved until you've been loved by God.

up because we stayed stuck on stupid. We missed our exit off Fools' Freeway in this bad relationship. Check this: God is so good that when God starts loving on you, God's love is healing. That's why the Bible says that when Jesus died for us, he was wounded for our transgressions and bruised for our iniquities (Isaiah 53:5, KJV). But then the verse says, "with his stripes we are healed." That's the kind of love God gives you. When God loves you, God's love will heal your past hurts.

Third and finally, when God loves you, God's love will *take you places* you never dreamed of. Don't you love that God tells Abram, "I know you're old, but I'm going to take you and make you the father of a great nation. I love you so much I'm going to take you places you've never dreamed of" (see Genesis 12:2). Isn't that good news today? When God loves you, God will take you places. But be prepared for some surprises along the way, because God's love is faithful—*and* unpredictable!

29. Mission Possible

To me it's a horrible thing to wake up in the morning with nothing to look forward to. It makes life so much more miserable if you wake up saying, "I don't know what I'm going to do today." How does one make it just going through the motions, settling for the same-old same-old?

I've discovered that life itself will drive you crazy with its ups and downs, highs and lows, good days and bad days. But you have to have the sense to recognize that God has sent you here for a mission. And guess what. If God sent you here for a mission, it is a mission that is possible.

The late, great Dr. Benjamin Elijah Mays, who was the sainted mentor of the one and only Martin Luther

**If God sent you here for a mission, it is
a mission that is possible.**

King Jr., put it this way. He said, "To be able to stand
the troubles of life, one must have a sense of mission
and the belief that God sent him [or her] into the
world for a purpose to do something unique and dis-
tinctive, and that if he does not do it, life will be worse
off because it was not done." What a powerful statement. Dr. Mays was declaring that you have a mission—and with God your mission is possible. But
what does that mean?

I'll give you three answers to that question. First,
Dr. Mays was suggesting that you are no accident. You
are here with intent, so live every day *on purpose*. Don't
you love that? You're no accident; you were sent here by
God with intent, so every morning wake up on purpose.
Walk on purpose. Think on purpose. Talk on purpose.
Work on purpose. Why? Because you are a person *preg-
nant* with purpose.

Second, Dr. Mays said, "Everything you go through
is setting the stage for what you were meant to do."
You *have* to love that, because in a sense we all go
through hell. We all have bad days when we feel cast
down, but check this. God is using all that negative
stuff to set the stage for what it is we are meant to
accomplish in this life; God is putting something in you.

As you are going through, God can get something done through you.

Finally, since you have a mission that is possible, you had better recognize the world is waiting on you to do what you are meant to do. My question is, what are you waiting for?

30. Would You Please Make Your Point?

Have you ever been in a conversation with someone who was pointless, and you just wanted to holler as they were talking, "Please, make your point"? Listening to people who are all over the place and making no sense can work your last nerve.

I've discovered that a lot of folks are living their whole *lives* like that. They are all over the place, but their lives make no sense because their life isn't making a point. My question is, Does *your* life make any sense? The answer depends on the point you are trying to make. The question of today is simply, what is your point?

When you look at your life, when you look at what you are about, when you look at your purpose, *what is your point*? You see, the point of a conversation is the goal of the discourse—to persuade, entertain, or inform. What is the purpose, or goal, of your life? I ask the question because my desire is that you would live a life where you make your point.

Why? I'll give you three reasons. First, when you know *what* you are here for, there are some things you will not stand for. Whenever you are making a point in a discussion, you become so focused on the point you are making that *side* issues cannot become *the* issue because you know what *your* issue is. Let me say that again. When you know what *your* issue is, you don't get thrown off by side issues. Why? Because you know what you are here for, and as a result, there are some things you will not stand for.

Second, if you know your purpose, you are connected to the Creator, and if you are connected to the Creator, everything you go through is just like a pencil sharpener. Life sharpens you so you can make your point better. Don't you like that? Whatever you are going through, those circumstances and situations are trimming away the stuff that's keeping you from making the point God intends for you to make. Everything you go through acts like a pencil sharpener. It's sharpening you so you can make your point.

Finally, knowing your purpose helps you stay on point. That's the last thing I want to tell you: *stay on point*. Yes, storms may come and winds may blow, but stay on point. Life may knock you down, but stay on

**Everything you go through acts like a pencil sharpener.
It's sharpening you so you can make your point.**

point. Haters may hate you, but stay on point. If you stay on point, God will ensure that your life *makes* your point.

That's how to make sense out of your life. First you have to answer the question, "What is my point?" And once you *know* your point, *make* your point. And once you start making your point, *stay* on point!

31. Enrolled in Resistance Training

Have you ever felt like so much was against you in life that you would never be able to make progress? Have you ever felt like, *Hey, everyone and everything is against me? This person is against me. I just don't have a chance. I have haters here, haters there. Here a hater, there a hater, everywhere a hater, hater. I have opposition here, and I have all these things that come up that are determined to set me back.* The bottom line is that all of us, if we're honest with ourselves, have felt those horrible days when it feels like everything or everyone is against us. I want to give you some good news: you've been enrolled in resistance training to overcome those days.

I was in the gym working out, and they had an advertisement for those who wanted to enroll in a special

...What's *against* you is being used by God to work out *for* you.

resistance training program. Basically, resistance training is a special program of lifting weights designed to go in the opposite direction of the way your target muscles are trying to go. If you are trying to push with your arms, the weights are designed to pull instead. In a real sense, the weights resist going where you're trying to go.

But guess what! It's through that resistance that you experience new strength, new power, and newly defined muscles. And it dawned on me, isn't God good like that? Every now and then when we think others are simply against us, God is using them as our specially designed weights, intended to strengthen us through resistance training.

Let me spin that out for you so you can capture what that means. One, what's *against* you is being used by God to work out *for* you. Isn't that good news? When you look back over your life at a lot of the stuff that was sho'nuff bad at the time, you will see that God used that stuff to work things out for you.

Two, the opposition that confronts you is being used by God to bring out the best in you. Isn't that good to know? That's why one writer said that the worst turns the best to those who are brave. If you look back over your life, much of your faith and strength have not come from simply going easily through life. They have come through over-coming the bad stuff! You didn't just *go* through those things; you were able to *grow* through those things. When you're going through your resistance training, please don't forget what the Bible tells us: that if God is for us, who can be against us (Romans 8:31)?

My word to you today is, when it seems like everything and everyone is against you, look at them and say, "Listen, you're simply my weights. God is using you for my resistance training."

32. No Time for Rubberneckers

One day I was driving along one of our city's freeways, taking my daughter, Abeni, to the mall. While driving on I-35, suddenly the traffic stopped flowing. The traffic was stop and go. Stop and go. Stop and go. We assumed there was a terrible accident ahead of us. However, by the time traffic was free to continue, we discovered that the real reason for the tie-up was an accident on the *other* side of the freeway—going in the opposite direction. We had been held up (watch this!) by rubberneckers who were looking at the accident and slowing up traffic.

My daughter, of course, had places to go, things to do, shopping to get done, and I will never forget her response: "Oh, we don't have any time for rubber-neckers." She was saying that rubberneckers slow down, look, and then move on about their business. And it dawned on me that so much is going on in the world today that we really don't have time for any rubbernecking. We have things to do and places we have to go, so we have no time for rubberneckers.

What do I mean, so much is going on? Check it out. There are accidents going on in the world. There's a humanitarian crisis where more than 180 thousand people have been killed in the Sudan and 2 million people are now homeless.

Check this: no time for rubberneckers. On a recent Sunday, the *Dallas Morning News* told the story of injustice experienced by a man named Tyrone Brown. Mr. Brown is in prison for life for stealing two dollars and violating probation for using marijuana.[1] There's no time for rubberneckers. Dallas has the highest crime rate of all big cities in the nation. It's no time for rubberneckers.

If all you do is look at what's going on and then speed up and move on about your business—if you don't take the time to step up and make a difference, then guess what. You ain't nothing but a rubbernecker. And since there is no time for rubberneckers, what does that mean? I'll tell you.

First, don't spectate but participate. The *blessed* of us have a responsibility to help the *rest* of us. It is one thing to go to church on Sunday and just shout about how blessed you are, how much favor God

The *blessed* of us have a responsibility to help the *rest* of us.

has shown you, how good God is to you. But if all you do is spectate but don't participate, then you aren't recognizing that your blessings aren't just about you. Your blessings are about what God will do *through* you.

That leads me to point number two. The God who's been good *to* you wants to be good *through* you, so look for ways to serve. Look for ways to get involved so you can make a difference. Write your representative in Congress. Call City Hall. Take a stand. Why? Because I've discovered that in the final analysis one person *can* make a difference.

Aren't you glad that when we look back in history we have a roll call of individuals who were just one but they made a difference? I'm glad Rosa Parks was just one, but she made a difference. Harriett Tubman was just one, but she made a difference. Martin Luther King Jr.—just one, but he made a difference. Jesus the Christ—just one, but he made a difference.

And all of those "just ones" resonate with the wonderful words of that song Dr. King often quoted, "If I can help somebody as I pass along, if I can cheer somebody with a word or song, if I can show somebody he's traveling wrong, then my living will not be in vain." What am I trying to say to you? There is a lot going on in the world. A lot of people are hurting; a lot of accidents are taking place. But Abeni put it like this: "Oh, we don't have time for rubberneckers." We ain't got no time for rubberneckers!

Note
1. Brooks Egerton, "Unequal Justice," *Dallas Morning News* (April 23, 2006). 1.

33. When Your Life Is Falling Apart

A while back I was watching the news on television, and the station showed a picture of two sinkholes right in the middle of a street. That would have been bad enough, but because of the sinkholes, nearby houses and swimming pools and all kinds of structures in that neighborhood had also given way and found themselves slipping, falling uncontrollably into the chasm of the sinkhole. Imagine how the inhabitants and homeowners of the community must have felt. It must have seemed like their lives were slipping totally out of control. Why? Because they were the victims of a sinkhole.

What is a sinkhole? Wikipedia defines it as "a natural depression or hole in the surface topography caused by the removal of soil or bedrock, often both, by water." In some regions, a sinkhole is caused by fluctuations in the water table, caused by drought or unusually heavy rainfall; some are formed when underground water eats away at a limestone layer beneath the earth's surface. In urban areas, a sinkhole may be formed when a water main or sewage line bursts.

Natural and human causes aside, I think that basically a sinkhole is a curse. Why? Because it demonstrates how what was once solid can become weak. It creates a fracture in a foundation, a gaping hole in what was once whole. Something beneath the surface, something underground, something that you could not see with the naked eye has been washed or drained away, and a sinkhole is the result.

Isn't that the way your life can be? Sometimes it seems as if life drains away those resources beneath our surface. Life keeps pulling on you and draining you, and after a while you feel as if you're falling into a sinkhole. The sinkhole syndrome makes you feel as though your life is sliding out of control.

What can you do when you find yourself in a sinkhole? First, learn how to call time-out. Life can be so fast paced that we find ourselves always on the go, always running. But every now and then you have to call time out. Why? Because there is no way you can have the interior resources to deal with those draining forces in life if you don't take some time out for yourself.

Second, keep a check on yourself so life won't sink you. If you don't take time out and keep a check on yourself,

**The sinkhole syndrome makes you feel as if
your life is sliding out of control.**

life can go bad. Here's a personal example: Recently I got sick. Why? Because my resistance was down. I did not keep a check on myself—on my physical and soul fitness—and as a consequence, life was able to sink me.

Finally, here's the good news. When a sinkhole comes, you know whom you can call, right? God specializes in rescue and revival. The Holy Spirit is always there for those of us who experience a sinkhole. When your life feels out of control because of a sinkhole, there is a God who is in control. Jesus is on the main line. Call him up and tell him what you need.

34. Quit Trippin' and Enjoy the Trip

My question of the day is, what are you worrying about? You see, I've discovered that worry will wear you down and wear you *out*. Anxiety will become like a cancer, and before you know it, anxiety's twin, fear, will leap into your mind and mess with your spirit, sabotaging from the inside out whatever it is you are trying to do. So the word of the day is quit trippin' so you can enjoy the trip.

I learned this lesson several years ago. I had to preach in Altus, Oklahoma, one Sunday afternoon, and that meant flying from Dallas–Fort Worth to Oklahoma City. But there was no flight to Altus in time, so someone volunteered, "We'll come get you on our private plane."

Well hey, I'm down with that because I'm having visions of Air Force One dancing in my head. Unfortunately,

Even when I cannot trace God's hand,
I can trust God's heart.

when they picked me up at Oklahoma City, it was not Air Force One. It was a little crop-duster plane. Really, just a small twin-engine plane. I wasn't feeling it when I was standing on the ground, but then we took off and experienced some bumpy weather. I was *sho'* not feeling it then!

That's when the pilot smiled at me and said, "How do you like my plane?" I think my face said it all. So he asked me, "But you're a preacher. Don't you trust God?" I said, "Yes, I trust God. It's just that I have more experience with God on the ground than I do in the air!" "Hold on," he told me. "If you really trust God and trust me, you'll simply fasten your seat beat and enjoy the ride." Then he said these words to me: "Quit trippin' and enjoy the trip."

That reminded me of a wonderful definition of worry I heard years ago from Dr. Harry S. Wright when I was a student at Bishop College. During a worrisome season for me, Dr. Wright said, "Worry is advance interest we place on troubles that may never come."

The pilot said, "Quit trippin' and enjoy the trip." Once I did that, I was able to look out the window and see the landscape, the beauty of the world God has created. And of course, the plane landed safely.

If we are going to enjoy this life, we have to quit trippin' and enjoy the trip. What lessons I pick up, I pass on to you!

First, I have discovered that adversity is an opportunity to bring out my creativity—and then show me some brand-new possibilities. That's why you shouldn't trip—because adversity is always an opportunity to bring out your creativity. And through those creative discoveries, you also unearth new possibilities you never saw before.

Second, I have learned to do what I can and trust God to do what I can't. Do what you can. That's all you can do anyway, so why are you trippin' on what you can't do? Do what you can, and then watch God step in and do what you can't do yourself.

Finally, I've learned that even when I cannot trace God's hand, I can trust God's heart. You see, I know God loves me. So even when I don't know what God is up to, I don't trip on it. I simply trust that God is doing what's best for me. Remember Paul who said, "Do not worry about anything, but in everything by prayer and supplication with thanksgiving let your requests be made known to God. And the peace of God, which surpasses all understanding, will guard your hearts and your minds through Christ Jesus" (Philippians 4:6-7, NRSV). The word of the day is quit trippin' and enjoy the trip.

35. Are You an Angel?

God knows the devil is always busy. And God isn't the only one who knows—all of us know. The devil is always busy, and he has a lot of employees who work for him. You've seen the devil's employees, haven't you? They bring drama into your life. They berate you. They hate you. They try to block God's blessings for you. Yeah, the devil is always busy, and to make matters worse, the devil has a whole lot of employees.

You could say the devil has no problem with unemployment. As a matter of fact, maybe if you're honest with yourself, you've probably worked for him part-time yourself. Yes, the devil is always busy, always trying to turn our lives upside down. Why, the very word *devil* is *lived* spelled backward. And, in a very real sense, if your life is backward, jacked up, torn up from the floor up, it's because the devil is always busy. And the devil has a lot of employees.

But isn't it great to know that "greater is he that is in you, than he that is in the world" (1 John 4:4, KJV)? So even though the devil has some employees, God has some angels too.

I was blessed one day while reading a story about a woman named Arletha Franklin in the paper. Arletha was one of those strong survivors from the city of New Orleans, and it so happened that she met some angels named Camille Rody and Katrina Runnels—Camille and Katrina. Don't forget those names! Arletha's family, including her three children and one grandchild, had survived hurricane Katrina and fled to Dallas. Shortly after arriving at Reunion Arena, they ran into Katrina Runnels. One day later they met Camille.

Now, of course, you know that Katrina was the name of the hurricane that devastated New Orleans, but Camille had been another devastating hurricane, one that flattened the coast of Mississippi in 1969. Isn't it just like God to make angels out of our hurricanes?

So Katrina and Camille were used by God as angels, and through their help, Arletha and her family found a place to stay, some money, and some food. Katrina and Camille became little angels to Arletha. Here's what Arletha said: "We laughed about their names at first, but it didn't matter whether their names were Katrina or Camille. They

Are you an angel? The answer depends on who you're working for!

were angels sent to help us. Isn't it good to know that angels are still operating, working for Almighty God?"

My question to you is: Are you an angel? Maybe you're hesitant to answer that because you aren't sure what angels do. I'm glad you asked! One, an angel is the *right* person at the *right* time who does the *right* thing for someone who is in the *wrong* situation, maybe about to do the *wrong* thing—even if that someone can't pay you back.

Two, an angel has a way of turning a negative into a positive, changing the bad into something good. Isn't that just what our girls Katrina and Camille did? They turned something negative into something downright positive.

Three, an angel in action sets off a heavenly reaction. When you do something positive for someone else, you are setting yourself up for angelic intervention in your own future. Why? Because what goes around has a way of coming around. The Bible calls it the principle of sowing and reaping. And that refers to the good you do, just as much as the bad. If you do good, I promise you that good is going to come back to you.

The question for the day is, are you an angel? The answer depends on who you're working for!

36. Be an Original

Many people are fooling themselves by not being themselves. As a consequence, they're not comfortable in their own skin, and they don't recognize the wisdom of "being what you is and not what you ain't."

A lot of times "we is what we ain't" because we're copying someone else. And—check this—whenever you try to copy someone else, you need to recognize that copies are not as good as the original. Sometimes people are not themselves because they're trying to be who they're not. Why? Because they're conforming to what someone else says they should be.

I was really blown away when I saw a picture of hip hop's class act, Mr. Kanye West, on the August 29, 2006, cover of *Time* magazine. The article inside talked about

> **[Keeping it real isn't] about conforming to what others say you should do; it's about conforming to what *God* says you should do.**

how Kanye is defying the rules of rap, going his own way, being his own man, keeping it real with himself. And there's my point—keeping it real means being true to yourself. It's not about conforming to what others say you should do; it's about conforming to what *God* says you should do. If you're keeping it real, it's not about going along with the crowd. It's about being who God has called you to be. It's about being an original. Kanye West is blowing up. Why? Because Kanye West understands the wisdom of keeping it real with himself—of being an original.

And that's my message to you. Be an original. Free yourself from what others think about you. Remember, God is not measuring you by someone else; God is measuring you by the you that God intended you to be.

I learned two things from that article on Kanye. First, no one can keep you from being the you that God meant you to be *unless you give them permission*. And second, when God made you, the Bible tells us the Lord said, "That's good" (see Genesis 1:31).

God made you. God patted himself on the back and said, "That's good." So be the you God made. Don't be less than you should be. Be an original.

37. Blowing Up When You Are Torn Up

You never really know what is in you until life puts the squeeze on you. When life puts on the squeeze, you find yourself in a tight space wondering how you are going to get out of whatever situation you find yourself in. Life has gone bad on you, things are going wrong for you, and nothing seems right in your world. We've all been there.

American poet Robert Browning said, "For sudden the worst turns the best to the brave."[1] Now let me give you the Freddie Haynes remix: When you are torn up, God blesses you to blow up. Here's an example. A while back, while working out with my good friends Robert and Dwain, we were talking about a trip Robert took. As pastor of All Nations Church, Garland, Texas, Rob had just returned from a mission trip in Brazil, and he

Even though wrong seems to have won the day,
good is on the way.

told us about a particular Brazilian flower that does not bloom in the daytime; instead, it blooms at night. Robert had questioned his tour guide about the flower, and the guide had explained that there was something about the night that brought out the beauty of this particular flower.

It dawned on me that this flower has a powerful testimony, because it's easy to bloom in the sunlight. Almost all flowers do that. It's easy to bloom when everything is going well. But this Brazilian flower says, "When all the lights are out and you cannot see your way, that's when I show my stuff. That's when I really blow up. Others might expect me to be torn up, but that's when I show off my beauty and blow up."

Isn't this what it means to be a child of God? Whenever you're going through the worst that life can send your way, isn't that when God somehow brings out the best in you? This "night flower" seems to show us that whenever life goes wrong and other folks want to write us off, God is still at work. Even though wrong seems to have won the day, good is on the way. That's what people mean when they say, "The best is yet to come." It is a call to recognize that God has a way of bringing the best out of you when life has done its worst to you.

The Bible tells us, "We know that all things work together for good for those who love God, who are called according to his purpose" (Romans 8:28, NRSV). So, when you have trials and tribulations, let faith work patience within you because the best is yet to come. You might feel as if you've been written off and torn up. But guess what. God is priming you and getting you ready. You're about to blow up!

Note
1. Robert Browning, from "Prospice" (line 21).

38. Now That I'm Hot, They All on Me

Rejected. Kicked to the curb. Dumped. Laid off. Dissed. Dismissed. Nothing can leave you doubting yourself and questioning your ability like being rejected and feeling unwanted. Rejection leaves you tore up from the floor up—feeling that you are not worthy of something you want or worthy of someone you desperately desire to be with. Rejection can come from any and every direction. It's there when you get laid off from your job. When your significant other dumps you. When your friend lets you down. When your family has turned their backs on you. How many times have you been good to somebody else and then that person turned around and treated you badly? That's rejection.

All of us know something about rejection. Have you

ever been passed over for a promotion on a job? You paid your dues. You played by the rules, and yet you got passed over. Can you testify to investing your life, your love, your heart, your hope into someone who left you for somebody else? Rejection hurts, but Mike Jones has something to say to all of us: "Back then they didn't want me, but now I'm hot, they all on me."

When you consider the lives of those who have done really well, those who have made a difference in our world, all of them can point to being rejected in the past by someone or something. For example, Luther Vandross sang four times at the Apollo Theater on amateur night and never won. *Back then they didn't want him, but now he's hot, they all on him.*

Anita Baker was told by several people not to give up her day job when she was trying to get a recording contract. *Back then they didn't want her, but now she's hot, they all on her.*

Michael Jordan, possibly the most famous professional basketball player of all time, was cut from his high school basketball team. Now he has six NBA championship rings. *Back then they didn't want him, but now he's hot, they all on him.*

The bottom line is this: Never allow rejection to define who you are, get in your spirit, and keep you from being everything God wants you to be. Remember these two things. First, if they reject you, they don't deserve you. Don't doubt yourself; doubt them. Don't doubt your taste;

When your life is in God's hands, rejection always sets you up for God's promotion.

doubt their taste. Evidently, they don't have a clue about all God has invested in you. Those who reject you are not worthy of you.

Second, when your life is in God's hands, rejection always sets you up for God's promotion. Look at Jesus! Scripture says Jesus was the stone the builders rejected, but now he is the chief cornerstone (see Psalm 118:22; Matthew 21:42). Jesus will testify "Back then they didn't want me, but now I'm hot, they all on me."

39. Not without a Fight

"You've been had. You've been took. You've been hoodwinked, bamboozled, led astray, run amuck."[1] Malcolm X uttered those famous words, but nowadays we would say, "You been punked." That's my daughter's favorite show on MTV: *Punk'd*. The sad thing is too many of us go through life getting punked. Tricked. Hoodwinked. Bamboozled. Why? Because we have adopted a victim's mentality. We allow stuff to happen to us as if we have no say in the matter. Then we go around blaming everybody else for why we don't have what we think we should have and why we are where we should not be.

You want to lose that victim's mentality. In your relationships, you think, *Nobody loves me. I'm a victim.* In

You have to make up your mind you're not going to be punked.

your career, you think, *Nobody wants to hire me. I'm a victim.* Listen, you have to make up your mind you're not going to be punked. You're not going to be a victim, not going to be had, hoodwinked, or bamboozled.

I was watching the NBC *Today Show* one morning, and some young girls were being interviewed. They were on the show because of a failed kidnapping attempt. Somebody had tried to kidnap them, and these girls had fought the kidnappers off. As a consequence, the girls were able to escape. Little girls—escaping kidnappers!

While interviewing the girls, Matt Lauer asked what lessons other people could learn from their experience. One little girl said: "Don't go down without a fight!" I like that. Don't go down without a fight. Don't be a victim. You won't go down without a fight if you can remember these three important points:

1. Nobody can make you a victim unless you give them permission. Don't give them permission!

2. Your life is worth too much for you to allow someone else to take you from you. Put a tag marked "priceless" on your life!

3. If God is for you, who can be against you (see

Romans 8:31)? Well, God is definitely on your side, so what do you have to fear?

So don't go down without a fight. Instead, do what the apostle Paul said in Ephesians 6:11, "Put on the full armor of God so that you can take your stand" (NIV). I don't know about you, but I'm no victim. I won't go down without a fight. Let's make sure that we stand firm.

Note
1. http://www.theblacknationalist.com/malcolmx.html (accessed May 5, 2007).

40. You Can Bounce Back

When life knocks you down, do you stay down, do you fall apart, or do you give up? When life throws that knockout punch, some of us throw a pity party, give in to despair, and go down for the count. Sometimes life knocks you down, and you just give up. You say, "Hey, this is it. I'm through." Then there are times when life knocks you down and you *can't* get up. You tell yourself you just can't take it anymore. As a consequence, you miss out on the new possibilities that come out of adversity. I'd like to encourage you today: You *can* bounce back.

I first learned this lesson from my daughter, Abeni, when she was twelve (going on thirty-two). Abeni was outside playing with a rubber ball, and she wanted me to play with her. She would throw it down and watch it bounce back up. And then she made a heavy statement. She said, "Daddy, the harder you throw it down, the higher it bounces back." That blew my mind, because it dawned on me that those who have been victimized, those who have been thrown down by terrible circumstances, need to know that the harder they go down, the higher they can bounce back.

When you throw down a plate, it breaks apart. And if you throw down a sandbag, it just thumps to the ground and stays there. But if you throw down a rubber ball, the harder you throw it down, the higher it will bounce back up.

I thought about the plate. I thought about the sandbag. And I looked at Abeni with her rubber ball. And I thought, *Sometimes when we get thrown down, we break apart like the plate. Sometimes we're thrown down and stay down, like the sandbag. But sometimes—check this—sometimes when we're thrown down, we bounce back even higher. What makes the difference?*

The difference between the plate, the sandbag, and the ball is in what they're made of. And it dawned on me that the same is true for us. How we respond to life's knockout punches depends on what we're made of.

I want you to know today that, if you love God like you should, you are made of some good stuff. And since you're made of good stuff, you *can* bounce back.

How do I know you're made of good stuff? Because the Bible says so. First, it declares, "Greater is he that is in you, than he that is in the world" (1 John 4:4, KJV). What does

How we respond to life's knockout punches depends on what we're made of.

that mean? That the God above you is also within you, and God is too great to allow what happens to you to have the last word on you.

Second, Scripture assures us that God "is able to do exceeding abundantly above all we can ask or think, according to the power that worketh in us" (Ephesians 3:20, KJV). What does that tell you? There is a power at work within you that says, regardless of what happens to you, the best is still to come for you.

So remember—when life throws what feels like a knock-out punch, that doesn't have to be the end of the contest. When you have God in your life, you *can* bounce back.